LOUIS
SULLIVAN'S

MERCHANTS
NATIONAL
BANK

BILL MENNER

Pomegranate

SAN FRANCISCO

Published by Pomegranate Communications, Inc.
Box 808022, Petaluma CA 94975
800 227 1428; www.pomegranate.com

Pomegranate Europe Ltd.
Unit 1, Heathcote Business Centre
Hurlbutt Road, Warwick
Warwickshire CV34 6TD, UK
[+44] 0 1926 430111
sales@pomeurope.co.uk

Front cover: Terra-cotta ornament on the façade, which otherwise suggests a simple
brick box. This burst of brilliance is one of Sullivan's best-known designs.

Back cover: The rose window creates a cathedral effect, with a maze of geometric and
organic shapes.

Library of Congress Cataloging-in-Publication Data
Menner, Bill.
  Louis Sullivan's Merchants National Bank / by Bill Menner.
        p. cm.
  ISBN-13: 978-0-7649-4040-8
  1. Merchants National Bank (Grinnell, Iowa) 2. Sullivan, Louis H., 1856-1924.
    3. Grinnell (Iowa)--Buildings, structures, etc. I. Title.

NA6243.G75M47 2007
725.2409777'596—dc22

                                          2006030677

Pomegranate Catalog No. A137

Book design by Lynn Bell, Monroe Street Studios, Santa Rosa, CA
Printed in Korea

CONTENTS

ACKNOWLEDGMENTS

Louis H. Sullivan made his mark on American architecture in places much larger than Grinnell, Iowa. His work in Chicago alone dwarfs his single contribution to this small town, which lies fifty miles east of Des Moines. Yet, for more than ninety years, Grinnell has been a destination for those who appreciate Sullivan's work, vision, and ornament. They flock to Grinnell to see the terra-cotta entryway, the Louis Millet–designed stained glass windows, and the stark juxtaposition of this simple brick box and its unparalleled ornament.

This celebration of Sullivan's masterpiece in Grinnell would not have been possible without the help of many people.

Grinnell College graduate David K. Kennedy of Racine, Wisconsin, took many of the photographs for this book. An appreciation of Sullivan's genius demands that his banks be viewed in full color, and David happily rode lifts and bucket-trucks to document that genius. He did this while completing his own book, *Portrait of Grinnell: The Architecture and Landscape of Grinnell College.* For more information about David and his work, visit www.david-kennedy.com.

Grinnellian Ivan Sheets shared his incomparable collection of historic postcards, which details the historic significance of Grinnell. Cheryl Neubert at the Grinnell College Archives provided support and guidance, while Larry Goodrich and Cindy Rose at the Grinnell Area Chamber of Commerce offered constant access to their office—the Sullivan bank itself. Mike Allen and Wells Fargo Bank have served as wonderful owners/stewards of the building. Wells Fargo also owns the banks in Owatonna and Cedar Rapids, so that company is vital to preserving Sullivan's legacy.

Photographer John Celuch of Edwardsville, Illinois, generously shared some of his images of Sullivan's other midwestern jewel boxes, a collection that has traveled across the region.

Malgosia Myc and Karen Jania at the University of Michigan's Bentley Historical Library secured the images of Sullivan's initial sketches of the bank, while Barbara Bezat and Alan Lathrop of the Northwest Architectural Archives at the University of Minnesota Libraries provided the terra-cotta shop drawings for the exterior façade.

Tim Samuelson, the city of Chicago's cultural historian and the world's greatest expert on Sullivan, has incredible insight into the bank. The time he provided was invaluable. Architect Michael Emerson of VOA in Chicago shared his experiences and appreciations restoring the Sullivan bank in Algona, Iowa. Society of Architectural Historians executive director Pauline Saliga opened the door to the Charnley-Persky House, the great 1892 Sullivan-Wright collaboration.

For the second time in four years, my family tolerated a book project. Once again, this is dedicated to my wife, Barb, and my children, Jack, Robbie, Ann, and Kate.

THE STORY OF
MERCHANTS NATIONAL BANK

On New Year's Day 1915, the community of Grinnell, Iowa, was basking in relative affluence. The town of six thousand featured Grinnell College, which had just turned out a group of graduates who would go on to shape President Franklin D. Roosevelt's New Deal. It was home to the Spaulding Carriage & Automotive Works, which just a few years earlier had been producing ten thousand buggies annually. Now Spaulding was turning out fine automobiles, one of which would defeat a "fast mail train" to win a cross-state race later that year. Grinnell also boasted a thriving central business district, many new homes, and an overall belief that things would get even better.

For architect Louis H. Sullivan, New Year's Day 1915 must have felt like a return to the glory days of his early career.

Called the "father of the American skyscraper," Sullivan helped forge a uniquely American architectural style and, in doing so, became the spiritual leader of the Prairie School. He had designed some of the most significant buildings in America and had already influenced a generation of architects. But, for Sullivan, the previous decade had been disastrous. Work had slowed to a trickle, and he was so deeply in debt that, in late 1909, he had been forced to auction off almost all his personal belongings. His physical health was beginning to decline, and he was increasingly frustrated by the lack of work. Sullivan's prospects, however, were improving.

On New Year's Day 1915, grand openings were scheduled for two of Sullivan's small-town midwestern banks: the tiny Purdue State Bank in West Lafayette, Indiana, and the Merchants National Bank in Grinnell. The Van Allen Department Store in Clinton, Iowa, and a third bank, the Home Building Association in Newark, Ohio, would open later that year.

Sullivan would design other great buildings, but he would never again see a year like 1915.

Louis H. Sullivan had an early interest in buildings, art, and design. He studied architecture briefly at MIT and Paris' École des Beaux-Arts before arriving in Chicago in 1875.

Louis Henri Sullivan was born in Boston in 1856 to immigrant parents; his father ran a dance academy, and his mother was a French tutor. Fascinated by buildings at an early age, Sullivan enrolled in the Building and Architecture program at Massachusetts Institute of Technology in 1872, when he was just sixteen. After a year at MIT, he spent brief periods working for renowned architects Frank Furness in Philadelphia and William LeBaron Jenney in Chicago. In 1874, he left for the prestigious École des Beaux-Arts in Paris.

Sullivan's formal educational experiences left him frustrated by the preoccupation with classical styles among practicing architects. He wanted to be creative, to blend design with both nature and art, and to create a style that was uniquely American. But Sullivan found those aspirations impossible under the formal rules of architecture stressed at MIT and the École. After spending less than a year in Europe, he returned in 1875 to Chicago. It was there, in the city that was still rebuilding from the great fire of 1871, that he would make his mark.

Sullivan's impact on both Chicago and American architecture is legendary. He and his partner Dankmar Adler designed the Auditorium Building—one of the greatest buildings of the nineteenth century—which was dedicated in 1889. The Transportation Building, designed for the 1893 Columbian Exposition, was stunning in both its size and its disregard for the classical styles that were prominent at the fair. The 1891 Wainwright Building in St. Louis, reaching eleven stories with a steel frame, marked the beginning of the modern skyscraper era. Sullivan would repeat that success with other skyscrapers in St. Louis, Chicago, Buffalo, and New York City.

Sullivan's personal approach to architecture, which he articulated in his essays and speeches as well as his building designs, was that a structure's outward form should express the function within. That concept—now known by the simple credo "form ever follows function"—is oft repeated by modern architects. But few supported Sullivan's ideas during his lifetime.

Although his partnership with Adler ended in 1895, Sullivan continued to design ground-breaking buildings, including the Chicago Stock Exchange and the Schlesinger & Mayer Department Store (now the Carson Pirie Scott Building) on State Street in Chicago.

By 1903, Sullivan's abrasive personality, coupled with a lack of business acumen, contributed to a decline in commissions. Despite receiving national acclaim for his designs, he had difficulty finding work, in part because he was an architectural purist. He believed his views on design were absolute and had little time for those who felt differently. In addition, he refused to follow the neoclassical trend that celebrated ancient styles. Sullivan felt his modern approach to design was the best approach for early-twentieth-century architects. But grand, classical designs were in vogue, and Sullivan's style was not.

Sullivan also favored an extravagant lifestyle, and the lack of work—and income—affected his quality of life. He had married in 1899, but he and his wife, Margaret, separated in 1909 as their financial situation grew more dire. He auctioned off most of his personal belongings that year, including his entire art collection, a letter from Walt Whitman, and expensive furniture. Sullivan received far less for his items than they were worth. Louis and Margaret never had children, and they divorced in 1917.

Nevertheless, Sullivan was getting some work. The president of a bank in rural Minnesota had read some of Sullivan's essays on architecture, design, and democracy. In late 1906, Carl Bennett hired him to design the National Farmers' Bank in Owatonna, Minnesota—the first of the "jewel boxes." Over the next fourteen years, Sullivan would design seven more jewel-box banks in small midwestern communities.

Benjamin J. Ricker was a Grinnell native and a graduate of Grinnell College. After leaving his hometown for a few years, he returned to work for the local glove factory, later becoming a co-owner. Ricker's wife was from Oak Park, Illinois—the town in which Frank Lloyd Wright, a former Sullivan employee, had established his studio and designed some of the first structures in what would become known as the Prairie School of architecture. Ricker likely became acquainted with that style, which can be traced to Sullivan's groundbreaking work of the 1880s and 1890s, through visits to his wife's hometown.

Wright worked for Sullivan from 1887 to 1893 before leaving to start his own firm. Wright, in turn, employed a talented young architect named Walter Burley Griffin. When B. J. Ricker was ready to build a new house on the north side of Grinnell, Wright was in Europe. So, Ricker hired Griffin to do the job. The Ricker House is considered the prototype for the Prairie School homes Griffin designed. In addition, Ricker was instrumental in the 1910 selection of Griffin to design a fountain in Grinnell's Central Park. Griffin's impact on Ricker would ultimately influence the corner opposite that fountain for decades to come.

Ricker served on the board of directors of Merchants National Bank in Grinnell, which by 1913 was looking for a new home. The bank was celebrating its thirtieth anniversary and needed more space. Ricker took on the task of finding an architect for the bank, but Griffin was unavailable; he was in Australia, designing the capital complex in Canberra. Ricker thus turned his attention toward Sullivan. He was clearly aware of Sullivan, through his influence on Griffin and through the publicity Sullivan was receiving for his other bank projects. Ricker and his fellow board members invited Sullivan to visit Grinnell.

Sullivan arrived in late November of 1913, met with the bank's building committee, and spent several days surveying the community, the central business district, and the corner he would work with at Broad Street and Fourth Avenue. He was absolute in his belief that there should be continuity between structures and their environment. In the case of downtown Grinnell, the environment featured adjacent two-story brick buildings, built in the 1880s, in the traditional commercial style of that era. Across the street to the east sat the town's iconic

Fourth Avenue Looking West, Grinnell, Iowa

918   C. U. WILLIAMS. PHOTOETTE BLOOMINGTON '

The site selected for the Merchants National Bank building in Grinnell, the northwest corner of Fourth and Broad, had featured a multistory commercial structure (foreground, at right) known as the "Grinnell Block," which dated to the 1880s. Half of it was razed for this project.

Courtesy Ivan Sheets Collection

14

ABOUT 1907

Broad Street north of Fourth, circa 1907. The Grinnell Block is at left.

Courtesy Ivan Sheets Collection

structure, the "Old Stone Church," home to the Congregational community that founded Grinnell. At the opposite corner was Griffin's fountain, and across the street to the south stood the "Phoenix Block," an 1889 collection of buildings designed by MIT-trained, Cedar Rapids–based architects Josselyn & Taylor in the aftermath of a devastating fire.

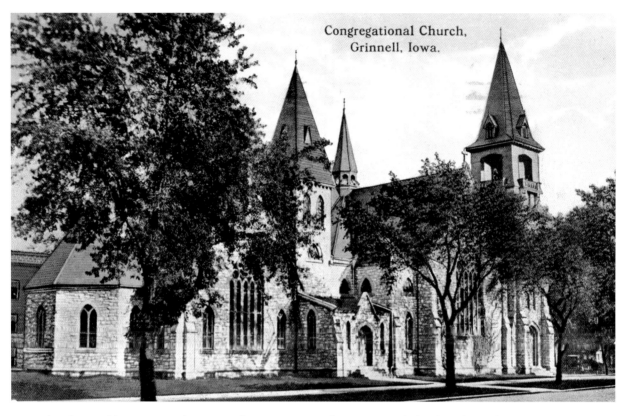

Congregational Church,
Grinnell, Iowa.

Sitting directly east of the site on Broad Street was the imposing Grinnell Congregational Church, nicknamed the "Old Stone Church." Built in 1877, it was the centerpiece of the community built by Congregational minister and town founder Josiah B. Grinnell. He was the person to whom newspaper publisher Horace Greeley allegedly imparted the advice "Go west, young man, go west."

Courtesy Ivan Sheets Collection

During his visit, Sullivan spent time in the city park—likely near the Griffin-designed fountain—mulling his options for Merchants National Bank. His sketches from that time show minimal variation on the jewel-box theme from initial concept to final product. Sullivan did much of the sketching in a room adjacent to the bank president's office. The bank's entire board of directors had intimate knowledge of the sketches as they progressed.

The two-story brick cube would feature prominent stained glass facing east, toward the Old Stone Church. Stained glass was a common characteristic of Sullivan's banks. But he immediately identified a critical ornamentation that would distinguish the Grinnell project—an intricate terra-cotta entrance built around a cathedral-like window.

In 1916, Sullivan would describe his design experience in Grinnell to fellow architect Andrew Rebori, who documented it in an article for *Architectural Record.* In "An Architecture of Democracy," Rebori recounted Sullivan's process. "For three whole days he talked, drew, rubbing out as changes were made, fitting and adjusting to the satisfaction of all. . . . I asked Mr. Sullivan how it happened that his preliminary sketches were worked out in such definite manner, and he answered quite simply that 'those were the requirements as given, and it only remained to jot them down on paper.'"

In fact, Sullivan did just that, using a notepad of yellow legal paper purchased from the drugstore located next to the building site. Working drawings were done by the end of February 1914, and construction began. Ten months later, on January 1, 1915, the doors were opened to the public. The bank had cost sixty thousand dollars to construct.

The bank's exterior featured tapestry brick, giving it a multicolored hue. The stained glass on the east side provided a primary source of natural light to the interior. It also linked the building to the rest of the Broad Street block to the north. Sullivan added two small, rectangular office windows at street level to the front of the building—elements that almost go

DR E W CLARK MEMORIAL
GRINNELL, IA. -125-

Architect Walter Burley Griffin, a protégé of Frank Lloyd Wright, designed the fountain that stood at the southeast corner of Fourth and Broad. Griffin also designed a house in Grinnell for Benjamin Ricker, who led the architect selection process for the Merchants National Bank board of directors. Sullivan likely viewed the bank site and sketched his initial concepts while sitting by this fountain.

Courtesy Ivan Sheets Collection

unnoticed when considering the façade as a whole. The dominant theme was the rose window medallion, using overlapping circles and squares to create something that looks like a shield. The accompanying terra-cotta ornamentation also used squares, circles, and botanical forms, extending the relationship.

For this project, as with many others in his career, Sullivan turned to Kristian Schneider to design the molds for his terra-cotta ornaments. Schneider was a Norwegian immigrant craftsman who worked for the American Terra Cotta & Ceramic Company outside Chicago. Schneider had first worked with Sullivan on the terra-cotta in the Schiller Theater project in Chicago. From that point in 1893, Schneider learned to work from the very simplest of small scale drawings with no need for details. He could not originate designs, but his skills as a craftsman were unparalleled. The magnificent terra-cotta ornament in the National Farmers' Bank was Schneider's, as were the features at the Woodbury County Courthouse in Sioux City, Iowa, a masterpiece of Sullivan's protégé George Elmslie.

The stained glass, as well as the mosaic surrounding the clock on the south interior wall, was the creation of Louis Millet, another longtime Sullivan collaborator. Millet played a major role in Chicago's vibrant art scene of the late nineteenth and early twentieth centuries. In 1893, he founded the Chicago School of Architecture, a multidisciplinary degree program offered jointly by the Art Institute of Chicago and Armour Institute of Technology. A highly respected professor of decorative design at the Art Institute, Millet also bolstered the American Arts and Crafts movement by preparing many talented students—predominantly women—for successful careers in the industrial arts.

Millet's stained glass creations gave the bank's interior an ever-changing feel, depending upon the date, time, and weather. They also helped Sullivan create a cathedral-like tone inside the commercial space.

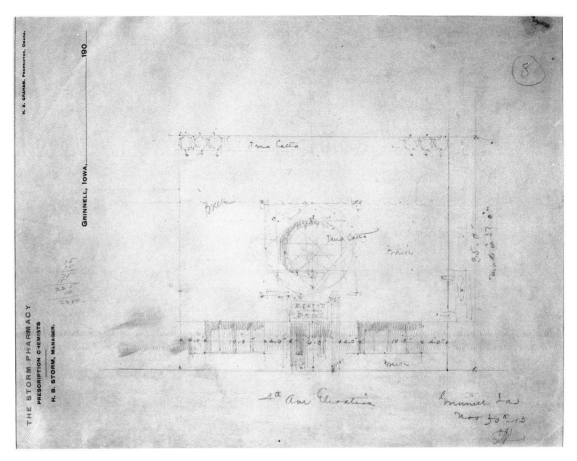

During a visit to Grinnell in late 1913, Sullivan purchased a yellow legal pad at a downtown drugstore to begin sketching his ideas for the bank. Working closely with the bank's board of directors, he developed a plan that changed remarkably little from conceptualization to implementation. This sketch shows the famed ornamental design that would define the building.

Courtesy Bentley Historical Library, University of Michigan

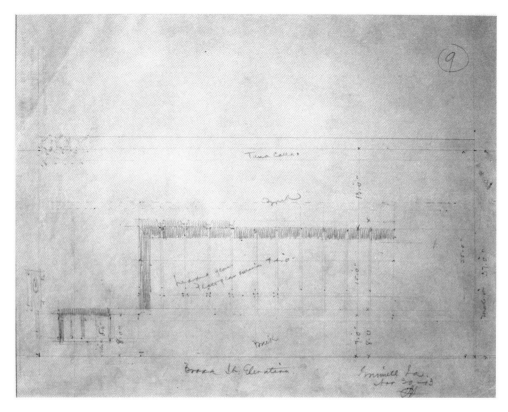

Sullivan's sketch showing the proposed site elevation.
Courtesy Bentley Historical Library, University of Michigan

Doubts had been voiced throughout the community during the ten-month construction, but they vanished once the project was completed, replaced by praise for features ranging from access to public telephones and restrooms to the ventilation system that constantly circulated fresh air. There arose a broad understanding that Sullivan had created something very special in Grinnell.

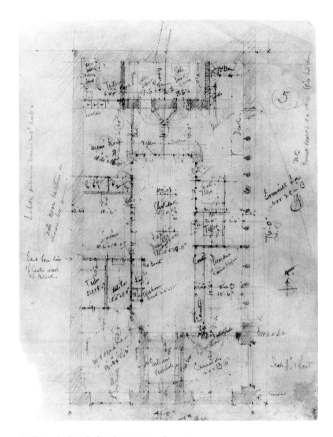

Sullivan's sketch for the interior layout.

Courtesy Bentley Historical Library, University of Michigan

A reporter from the *Grinnell Herald* was permitted a preview, which he detailed in a long, glowing article that appeared in the paper's December 28, 1914, issue.

Next Friday evening, the officers of the Merchants National Bank invite their friends in to see their new banking room. For the best part of a year, we have been watching the erection of the building from the outside; have criticized, favorably or otherwise, the plain lines of the long, high one-story building, the large window on the east, the ornamental front, even the golden-winged lions which guard the portal of the bank's new home.

In his review, the reporter was clearly mesmerized by what he had seen. The article alludes to the *Arabian Nights* and Persian fire worshippers, hinting that Sullivan's immersion in Near Eastern culture must have "worked like hashish." But, as the reporter acknowledged, the vision that emerged was sheer genius.

The architecture of Merchants National Bank building is to represent strength, security and wealth. When walking through it, notice the

pains which have been taken with details regardless of expense. The design of the ornamenta-
tion of the terra cotta and the woodwork . . . was drawn originally for this building. The figures
in the front glass window were drawn by Mr. Sullivan and colored by Millet, a relative of the
great French artist. The effects in the lower half of the building are obtained by the use of Roman
brick, marble, bronze and quarter-sawed oak: and the fairest of these is the quarter-sawed oak.
The entire floor is of pink Tennessee marble, the walls halfway up and the counters are of brick.
Where the counters are topped by a bronze grill, it means that space is reserved for the officers
and employees of the bank.

Another writer described the opening with equally awestruck prose.

The new Merchants Bank building is not a mere building. It is a creation. It was realized first
in the mind of Louis H. Sullivan. Mr. Sullivan dreamed the building. The building is his dream
come true.

The most common sentiment expressed by the hundreds of visitors who squeezed
into the bank on the evening of January 1, 1915, was quite basic: "This does not look like
Grinnell." The *Grinnell Herald* reporter warned his readers that a cursory tour of the building was not sufficient.

Go back to the north end and turn around to the south. Raise the eyes above the partitions and
brickwork and catch the massive simplicity of the long beams along the ceiling: study the win-
dow colored by Millet and its mosaic replica below which surrounds the clock with face of gold.
Raise the eyes still higher to the skylight. . . . If you are in just the right mood in time you can
hear the dash of the waters over Niagara Falls, listen to the winds that sweep across the prairies
of the West, see the blue that hovers over the land of the azure sky and understand something of
what Sullivan meant when he talked about the genius of America.

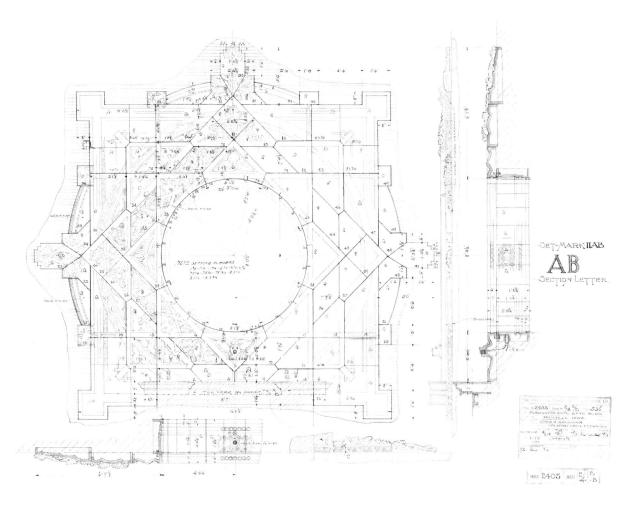

Sullivan worked closely throughout his career with the American Terra Cotta & Ceramic Company near Chicago, which produced most of his stunning architectural terra-cotta ornament. These shop drawings provide a piece-by-piece map for the bank's historic façade.

Courtesy Northwestern Architectural Archives, University of Minnesota

MERCHANTS NATIONAL BANK.
GRINNELL. IOWA.

The bank took less than one year to build and opened to the public on January 1, 1915. Sullivan sought to fit the building into its surroundings, hence the roofline that matches the adjoining structures. While the bank does feature gilded ornament, the colorized artistic postcard exaggerates the gilding.

Courtesy Ivan Sheets Collection

M
E
R
C
H
A
N
T
S

N
A
T
I
O
N
A
L

B
A
N
K

G
R
I
N
N
E
L
L

I
O
W
A

"CHILD"

The Merchants National Bank created a sensation in Grinnell because it was unlike any other commercial structure in the city. Postcards of the bank were plentiful, including this pair showing the bank's interior. One card (above) looks to the front of the bank, highlighting the rose window; the other (opposite) looks to the rear and the vault.

Courtesy Ivan Sheets Collection

"CHILD"

Seen next to its neighboring structures, the bank stands out as being far ahead of its time.

Courtesy Ivan Sheets Collection

THE BANK TODAY:
A PHOTO GALLERY
PHOTOGRAPHS BY DAVID KENNEDY

The buildings originally adjacent to the bank are gone, but Sullivan's structure still commands the northwest corner of Fourth and Broad. The city has re-created the geometric shape of the bank's façade with brick pavers in each downtown intersection.

The explosion of terra-cotta ornament almost overwhelms the façade, which otherwise suggests a simple brick box. This burst of brilliance is one of Sullivan's best-known designs. Once-gilded griffins still guard the entrance to the building.

31

The ornamental details of Sullivan's design and Kristian Schneider's terra-cotta handiwork appear in this view looking upward from street level.

An eye-level view of the rose window shows its overlapping geometric shapes and the complexity of Louis Millet's stained glass.

Sullivan's ornamental design featured gilded highlights, drawing the eye upward some twenty feet above street level.

The intricacy of the ornamental frieze surrounding the rose window is organic to the accompanying geometric framework.

The brown terra-cotta cornice features small finials that provide a roofline flourish. A thin band of similarly colored terra-cotta provides a base at sidewalk level.

The east-looking griffin is one of a pair protecting the terra-cotta entry. More organic design elements can be seen in the doorway, while Fourth Avenue extends to the west.

The iron plaque above the doorway notes "Louis H. Sullivan, Architect." This street-level look upward shows nicely the complexity of the façade and ornamental elements.

Although the grates that defined the tellers' windows were removed, the bank's interior has otherwise changed little since 1915. The check desk still anchors the center of the floor.

Sullivan's design made extensive use of natural light, with stained glass in the east wall, the rose window, and the skylight. The atmosphere within the bank changes almost hourly due to the diversity of color in the glass.

Merchants National Bank is a Sullivan masterpiece, but it also features the spectacular work of Chicago artist Louis Millet, a frequent Sullivan collaborator. Millet's stained glass and clock mosaic add color and complexity to the interior.

The rose window creates a
cathedral effect, a recurring theme
in Sullivan's "jewel boxes." A maze of
geometric and organic shapes, the window
creates a sunburst effect on midwinter mornings.
During this time of the year, the sun, low in the sky, lines
up with the window and fills the bank with brightly colored light.

Millet's glass mosaic was assembled in his Chicago studio, shipped to Grinnell, and installed.

The check desk that anchors the bank floor is an organic marvel. The meticulous hand-carved design appears to grow out of the marble floor in an explosion of ornament.

The monumental stained glass windows on the east wall stand fifteen feet high and forty feet wide. Highlighting their exterior are once-gilded iron columns. Of double thickness, the windows feature plate glass on the exterior and leaded glass on the interior. Millet's work allows natural light to create a multicolored array on the bank's bare opposite wall.

As in many Sullivan designs, organic figures populate the ornament. They also serve to accentuate the spiritual, cathedral-like quality of the bank's interior.

The natural light that floods into the building comes from the windows to the east and the skylight above, as well as the rose window.

Gold-colored terra-cotta—molded and crafted by frequent Sullivan collaborator Kristian Schneider—re-creates some of the organic figures occurring elsewhere in the bank.

THE OTHER BANKS

Merchants National Bank in Grinnell was the fourth of Sullivan's so-called jewel boxes, a name he coined. The first, completed in 1908, was the National Farmers' Bank in Owatonna, Minnesota. It helped revitalize Sullivan's flagging career, although it did not have the impact it should have had. It did, however, lead to jobs in the Iowa communities of Cedar Rapids, Algona, and Grinnell. The Grinnell bank opened the same year as banks in West Lafayette, Indiana, and Newark, Ohio. A bank in Sidney, Ohio, and the eighth and last, the Farmers & Merchants Union Bank in Columbus, Wisconsin, would follow.

These eight stunning buildings—with trademark brick-box simplicity and organic ornamentation—capped Sullivan's remarkable career. They demonstrate perfectly his approach to structure, context, and ornament, while allowing personal statements about capitalism and agrarian ideals.

Sullivan went on to design a façade for the Krause Music Store in Chicago in 1922, but he never completed a full building project after the Wisconsin bank. During the final years of his life, he survived, to a large degree, on financial handouts from friends. Although penniless, he remained in regular contact with Dankmar Adler's son, as well as Frank Lloyd Wright and other colleagues, who helped pay Sullivan's bills. Louis H. Sullivan died in his sleep in a Chicago hotel room on April 14, 1924, of kidney disease. He was sixty-seven.

(opposite) Detail of terra-cotta ornamentation on The Peoples Savings & Loan Association in Sidney, Ohio.
Photograph by John Celuch

Sullivan's first "jewel box," the National Farmers' Bank (1908) in Owatonna, Minnesota, anchors an important downtown intersection. Its thirty-six-foot-wide arches dominate the exterior, while its terra-cotta, stucco, cast iron, and marble elements create a symphony of colors. The organic terra-cotta ornament (opposite) seems to celebrate Sullivan's return to national prominence and set the stage for the seven banks to follow.

Photographs by John Celuch

The Peoples Savings Bank (1911) of Cedar Rapids, Iowa, is highlighted by four corner towers of a tall, central banking hall surrounded by a wider, single-story base. The building is nearly devoid of ornament, in part due to budget constraints, but natural light and stained glass are prominent features.

Photographs by John Celuch

The Henry C. Adams Building (1913) of Algona, Iowa, features Sullivan's trademark tapestry brick, produced by raking and firing each brick differently so it ends up with unique texture, hue, and color saturation. The result is striking compared with buildings employing uniform glazed brick. The rectangular Adams building was designed as a bank but opened as a real estate office. Its simplicity is enhanced by the brickwork and selected terra-cotta ornament.

Photographs by John Celuch

The Purdue State Bank (1915) of West Lafayette, Indiana, opened the same day as Sullivan's Grinnell bank. The smallest and least expensive of the jewel-box banks, it had to fit into an unusual triangular lot. Sullivan designed a trapezoid building featuring multicolored tapestry brick with green glazed terra-cotta around its stained glass and entry.

Photographs by John Celuch

The Home Building Association (1915) of Newark, Ohio, is a two-story building designed to house a large operation. It was the only one of the jewel-box banks to feature terra-cotta as a covering material rather than tapestry brick. The gray base allowed Sullivan great opportunity for using color in the ornamentation, including the glass mosaic over the doorway that spells out "the Old Home" in gold lettering.

Photographs by John Celuch

The Peoples Savings & Loan Association (1918) of Sidney, Ohio, is another simple rectangle made of tapestry brick. However, Sullivan's use of glass mosaic in the semicircle above the entry and above the towering wall of stained glass on the side makes this bank unique among the eight.

Photographs by John Celuch

The Farmers & Merchants Union Bank (1920) of Columbus, Wisconsin, was Sullivan's final "jewel box." He stayed in Columbus throughout the design and construction. Once again, tapestry brick is intensified by green glazed and brown terra-cotta. Anchoring the façade is a green marble panel that features the bank's name in gilded letters. Above it are two terra-cotta lions bearing shields. An eagle sits at the top, at the center of an organic frieze.

Photographs by John Celuch

71

LOUIS SULLIVAN CHRONOLOGY

1856	Born in Boston, MA.
1872	Attends MIT.
1873	Works briefly for famed architects Furness of Philadelphia and Jenney of Chicago.
1874	Attends École des Beaux-Arts in Paris; travels throughout Europe.
1875	Returns to Chicago; works as independent draftsman and designer.
1880	Hired by Dankmar Adler as draftsman.
1883	Promoted by Adler to full partner; Adler & Sullivan firm created.
1887	Frank Lloyd Wright begins six-year tenure as Sullivan's draftsman.
1889	Grand opening of Auditorium Building in Chicago propels firm to prominence.
1891	Eleven-story steel-frame Wainwright Building opens in St. Louis.
1893	Transportation Building resists neoclassical trend at Chicago's Columbian Exposition.
1895	Adler retires.
1898	Work begins on Schlesinger & Mayer (later Carson Pirie Scott) Store in Chicago.
1906	Hired to design National Farmers' Bank, Owatonna, MN.
1908	National Farmers' Bank opens.
1909	Completion of Peoples Savings Bank, Cedar Rapids, IA.
1913	Completion of Henry C. Adams Building, Algona, IA; bank design begins in Grinnell.
1915	Banks in Grinnell, IA, West Lafayette, IN, and Newark, OH, hold grand openings.
1918	Completion of Peoples Savings & Loan Association, Sidney, OH.
1920	Grand opening of Farmers & Merchants Union Bank, Columbus, WI.
1924	Dies in Chicago, IL.